I0078908

River Skin

Darcy Smith

Fernwood
PRESS

River Skin

Poems

©2022 by Darcy Smith

Fernwood Press
Newberg, Oregon
www.fernwoodpress.com

All rights reserved. No part may be reproduced
for any commercial purpose by any method without
permission in writing from the copyright holder.

Printed in the United States of America

Cover and page design: Mareesa Fawver Moss

Cover photo: Daniil Silantev via Unsplash

ISBN 978-1-59498-087-9

These are poems of invocation (*Come darkness come / it's time to break this tempest*), poems about nothing less than the way memories can swirl like a tilt-a-whirl, making what was blur and overlap. In these memories, the natural world keeps getting interrupted by switchblades of violence, yet the invocations (*dear silence come*), center us in the possibility of beauty.

—Nick Flynn,
author of *I Will Destroy You*

If one of the aims of poetry is to condense our vast, contradictory, and beautiful world into the briefest of songs, *River Skin* stands as a testament to its possibility. In these vibrant poems of landscape, family, and identity, Smith exhibits a true talent for imbuing natural, experiential detail with authenticity, layered meanings, and lyricism. But *River Skin* is so much more than that; it's also brimming with powerful meditations grounded in the familiar that eventually open us up to something far greater. It takes risks by exploring sincere, often harsh realities through rich, accessible language. These poems are intellectually stimulating and emotionally engaging, written by someone with clear eyes and an open, curious heart that shies neither from the darkness nor the light that, together, define the human condition.

—John Sibley Williams,
author of *As One Fire Consumes Another*

A train whistle, a smear of black ice, a mouthful of fishhooks—out of these nicked, glittering elements, Darcy Smith's *River Skin* transforms loss into "a torn place on [her] sleeve," a dwelling place in which, despite each vanishing, we remain. Smith is a poet of the cast and the lure, and although her poems singe the fingers, we are glad to be caught.

— Joshua Davis,
co-author (with Allison Blevins) of *Chorus for the Kill*

River Skin, Darcy Smith's first collection of poetry, roils through a downriver landscape of maple-lined roads, rust-covered tractors, and rose-wallpapered homes, its bucolic beauty casting the near-constant undercurrent of domestic trauma into high relief. Finely-honed and whetted, these are lines as sharp and clean as fishbones, pliantly molded into shapes both formal and inventive. Nouns masquerade as verbs, verbs as adjectives, scenes tantalize with fresh and surprising imagery, sonics tease, reverberate, and haunt. Moreover, these poems emanate tremendous empathy—a tender heart broken by a long procession of hard knocks. But like her river, Smith's skin is elastic, finding solace in the rustle of maples and oaks, the scent of lilacs, the wonder of lichens, the chatter of crickets, even the rust on the family tractor becomes salve for wounds. Read this book and marvel at how raw, angry fissures miraculously mend to become supple and glossy, time and again, as Smith stops to observe, harken, and honor them.

—Lissa Kiernan,
author of *The Whispering Wall*,
Glass Needles & Goose Quills, and *Two Faint Lines in the Violet*

Darcy Smith's *River Skin* examines, in exquisite language and vivid imagery, the many roles a woman may play in her life: as daughter, as sister, as wife, as mother. With each of these roles comes the challenging demands of love and the wounds we inevitably inflict on each other. "It only takes one thaw to end everything," Smith writes, and we feel the truth of this in her daring syntax and sharp eye. Still, despite the grief of addiction, of dying parents, of a stillborn birth, these poems are "sunless prayer[s]" and "greening hymns." They speak to the stony comfort of our own resilience, the way we can find a home amid ruins.

–Amie Whittemore,
author of *Glass Harvest*

Sean, Colin & Molly—my heart

Peg & Scott—my home

Galen, Bob, Stacey & Kenny—never forgotten

Josh, John, Mary, Nick, Lissa & Mare—deepest gratitude

Contents

What Color Cuts Bridles

If light leads a daughter to deep meadow green,
why does the air sink, like summer's last dream?
If fields wring the sky, red clover the clouds,
if night turns to day, tips silence too loud,

if scent leads a storm, petals ungotten,
if song leads a crab apple to blossom,
what is the taste of first hay in the heat?
What does a tractor tear down with its teeth?

Where does a cat land, no footing, all fours?
What opens eddies in trap cellar doors?
When dust motes bore potholes into my feet,
why did the mountain crawl under the sheets?

If swallows scream flurries out of my thighs,
if wind leads the heart to quicken to fly,
what has been taken, and why can't I see?
What color is broken, buried in leaves?

a towel hangs from a line
    a sheet of iron in the sky

Loose Gravel

I didn't ask these trains to howl me home,
to watch water slap steady on a pier of broken

pilings, soft like termite hills on the red-barn trail.
Gnats in the dead of summer, the river rips me
in her wake. Wait for the burst of maples. Sap

runs and red crisps, a bushel fresh picked.
Half-eaten core, tossed to the tracks before

the glaze of an autumn rain. I scramble out
from a bank of loose gravel, dust and screams could

be a kettle or maybe Ma cursing the empty
cupboard. I didn't ask. The train howls me back

to red crisps, fresh picked. As if I could forget
bobbing for a Gala in a ghost sheet. Mouth wide,
a wet grab, almost finding. As if I never learned how

to throw out a mealy apple. I know where bushels get ground,
pulp almost too sweet, after the root cellar, after they leave.

If You Meet My Father

I won't explain the chartreuse drips across his canvas nor
the pinky ring—do you see the salmon shirt he adores

more than Pollock? And the socks he hunted
all of Florence for instead of gaping at the David?
The perfect cashmere orange pink.

I won't explain his need to match, nor his love
of a well-built sandwich. Did he give you a nickname yet?
Win his heart, hate your tag—he won't care

to change it or you, and when I say, *Hey Dad, you have a guest,
so don't swear too much. For you,* he says, *I can fucking do that.*
He hugs too tight, you inch away, but know as I do now

that, like his garnet and his action painting,
he mixes you in oils that don't wash out.
You are the frying pan, roast beef on rye,

you are his Pollock, his extra mustard, perfect salmon-
matching socks, you are his David clad in cashmere.

On the Pond

all the kids steered clear of black ice.
My brother's thick blades scraped
beneath snow-pitched pines. Skirting

fractured seams, he sped past me
like our barking spaniel, snagged
by the scent of a woodchuck.

He fled jagged silence and the snap
of our father's belt for the solace
of hustlers and smack.

Like our dog, he came home
stinking of the entrails he rolled in,
one fix following another.

He left
before the thaw, ice
spitting behind his blades.

Did You See Him

in every mirror   did you
       hear him   behind each door another coat
your lips red orange   painted courage cracked
     when your son   left you
didn't dare ask or dig past   his veins collapsed

       he moved on   clefting the web
    of skin between   his toes.

     Your new slipcovers
       brightened the living room,
         which was never truly warm.

    He came back
     woodstove   gone cold
  seizing not quite   convulsing
   spit gurgling   not throwing up not

that there's ever   any noise when
winter nights turn black   his eyes
       rolling   past
      then back   to you
        and Dad   then I got shooed
          back   to bed
         shivering.

Fresh Eggs for Mama

I called you Venus. We laughed, applied deodorant
to the thin of your world, pillows propped, a pasture of hens.
You wore 89 degrees and nothing more because
at 92 you give in—to my basin of soapy water,
another pair of underpants soaked, though
the cushions dry fast enough.

There is a hornet in the room,
and one of us will have to slap

the screen door shut. Strands of our grays,
dead wings—stuck like an ice pack I shimmied
into the angry splotch again. I can't eat—
your demands, grinding gums. I floss
the edges of a windless night, and even politics
taste mild. Your accident cried me here without
a poem because I knew you wouldn't like the smell.

There is a hornet in the room,
and one of us will have to warm

your broth, crooked straw and pills
to pull the pain up a long-forgotten rope
hung from the maple. I count drips of daylight.
Your eyes make watermarks, each inch of me
stamped. I lift you to the toilet, strained
groans; we hold each other's armpits.

There is a hornet in this room.
One of us will have to go.

Skate Me a River

—I would teach my feet to fly. Joni Mitchell

River ice holds most anything—
Ma's station wagon, Dad's tractor, the nasty
vacuum, your bed, a barge bound to break

mountains of their sheen. You know it
only takes one thaw to end everything—
blue jeans, double layered and damp,

work like triple socks. Don't ask why
Dad comes home late. You trust

knotted laces, used skates.
Ice boats are dragon shimmer,
a skitter you can trace,

like your breath pushing itself,
a white plum floating over—
everyone is laughing like the sun

splashing a milk-sweet flurry. If he
upends the coffee table,
don't complain; you shouldn't

but you have to—
ask it's six o'clock. Ma hands you
the phone. Call the bar again. Set the table.

He didn't see you half asleep,
his raised suitcase. Rivets
pop   if you   pull

worn laces too tight. Truss them
just so. He packed his bag once.
When you skate on the river, you trust

you won't fall in because ice boats
mean cracked leather is safe
even when your toes go numb.

In Folded Stone, I Find You

You were my aquifer. I am your limestone
cleaving these catacombs. Let me rest

in honest darkness. Hush now, Sister,
how your broad laugh lingers. Bring me

the comfort of stone,
damp walls, half shadow.

This cool dirt quells. I believe
in deep time, in the promise

of my mutt's paws, in the branching
decades between us, tethered like our

tire swing, like our maple,
pleached to a forgotten

scythe. My thin rings, our bright
rust. I am sunless prayer. Shade

me from these lilacs, from their insistent
clamor. Quiet the exaltation of apple trees,

endless greening, robins, snow-stained
tulips. Bring me a steady rain,

the patter of our one-two puddle
jump. Your smile, eager like my pup's

first bray. Roll me in warm fur, fetch me
new skies. Leave me to this pounding

joy, this sting of morning. Our summers,
a gnawed frisbee in the soft of his mouth.

What Lingers

We are green laughter
    butter sun rolling
        our backs
           tumble mare tails

    swells of clover
        grassy knoll, no rocks.
          We are the breeze
            that ripples dandelion.

a piece breaks off,
    declares itself

Before We Burned

your photograph, I tore myself
out of the picture. We scattered you
into the sea. Dearest sister, yield
your ash to this wind, lost gulls, gray sun.

Dog Flowers

I can't bring her back
can't outrun this snarling

hound, his hungry
snap won't stop

my missing
can't mend this gashing

can't bring her home
can't brush her hair.

Why bother with fresh-cut
flowers everywhere?

These petals fester
past forever, past barking,

past wilting, past flooding
blood lilies churning

bouquets in every room
can't fix her days are

never

throw them out, don't—
touch her

flowers. Don't.
Don't you see?

We all turn
a shade of red.

Skimming Stones

Mountains hound me,
their silence—honeyed, endless.

I stomp the hard ground,
another life gone, water rips—

toss stones against
the pitted water barrel.

Abundance, We Beseech You

Mother, bring us greening hymns
                    our seedlings quiver.

Come sing us a lullaby
              our brook falls silent.

We pray, leaf and storm
              cupped petals calling.

Mother, hold close these nestlings
                    their outstretched mouths—

Sing us your katydids, crickets,
                broken leaves, bud song.

Egg Shells

This sea, this labor, unrelenting.
My breath, an anchor. *He-He-Who.*
He-He-Who. He-He-Whooo.

She speaks in glances,
coaches through quivering, through
cresting breath and sweat.

My husband hovers with orange juice,
protein bars, an unlit candle.
Breathe with me or get out.

He-He-Who. He-He-Who. He-He-Whooo.
An anesthesiologist, mask in hand.
Just breathe. Normally.

I'm a little loopy, have no idea why.
Someone has to tell the mother. I slip
into Nana's kitchen. She blankets

her table with flour, sun specks, powdery
waterfall. She builds a center well, pulls an egg
from her apron, faded roses, torn pocket.

Yolk dives slippery,
cracked shells linger,
empty and open.

Nana coaxes shape
where there was none. I wake
to a nurse's tender steps,

her face ruddy, swollen. My eyes
beg. She shakes her head,
holds my hand. Dawn hangs

between us,
open, empty.

Jellyfish in June

An ocean of shadow circles
me like carrion, cawing my chest
hollow as a horseshoe crab that held
a heart, lungs and blood. The husk, shored
without a pulse. This beach, my breath, held fast.

Your Lilacs Nest in Me

—And your very flesh shall be a great poem. Walt Whitman

I give you a constant breath behind
the door. I give rusted hinges,
unsprung locks. I give you my sprig of lilac.
I give you the earth breached. I give you endless,
hopeful, airless heat. I give you wet
smoke. I give you the waning sun.

Let me in your spider's web. Let me stick
to the center of forever spinning, pouring
my hair falling from a willow's arms. Let me
lay my sprig of lilac at your feet. I give you
a song, myself. I give you the gnawing need
to be the woods that listened you.

Pluck a mint leaf. Make me your morning
tea. I'll hide inside the rim, sip the silver edge
of empty, but for your mud-slicked evenings,
for your tumbled sighs, for the stranger's eyes,
in shoulders cresting, in arms glistening, in each
shattered second, a stifled gaze.

Come now, Walter, you must see Vincent
born in you. It's just a book; see how his oils sing,
binding me to you, to ribbons torn from within?
Let me open Vincent's nests, hidden
in this book I use to cover the soft
nicks of my father's table. Take my sprig of lilac.

Take my blistered cries, my cheap whiskey, my want
of what is not written, green sonnets, air-dried stacks,
unseen stanzas, oils mixing me as Van Gogh does,
screaming in my ear, his severed galaxies inside
my mouth. As if he speaks only motion, as if you
speak me inside his needled light,

inside his cell, inside San Remy, inside my thinning
silence, inside his cypress. He brought bird nests in the hollow
of night, he was twigs breathing, he was saliva
from a robin's breast. The spider silk he threw,
a knotty white, one tone pulsing on moss drying,
on glinted black, the brambles he snapped

the wind, warped bars wobbled my throat, you warbled me
into his star-spun sea, into your trailing phrases, into hayfields,
into nights starred into unmetered longing. My eyes scalded
for want of an iris opened, for want of one true line,
for the spell his nests cast on my every broken branch.
Keep my sprig of lilac.

Durable Spring Bulbs

I

Larkspur—
carry me on
bareback winds. Gallop past
past time's broken swings. August hayfield,
scorched rain.

II

Why would
Apollo send
me his last hyacinth?
Petals, a brittle blue. The sun's
torn too.

III

Black-eyed
Susans, buckled
over. Path to rehab—
make me your footbridge, lay me down
again.

IV

Why did
I pick an oak?
Lullabies can't be un-
sung. Autumn grays me like your ash,
small bones.

Your Name, Galen

—means peaceful, calm and healer

Perhaps I die with you in increments;
I believe
in long wounds.

What use have I
for the scratch of a suckled moon?
I believe

binding eases
breasts once wet. How do tulips return
in the scratch of this suckled moon?

I'm carved and left
with your bassinet, the silence
of breasts once wet. How dare tulips return

without request, without a word
we speak
in decades' dust, your bassinet, the silence

of your cotton cap. We're cradled deep;
we're swaddled, still I die with you in increments.
We speak
in long wounds.

Petals

Walking a path of uneven bluestone,
wind bellows a spray of pink dogwoods.

Storm clouds plow under
the sunlit sky. I trample petals.

Screen door squawks. I set her dinner
on the kitchen counter. The living room,

a sea of linens on their sides. I sit at the edge
of a rented bed, her tired eyes, bag of urine.

The birds are loud today. She stares,
mouth slackens. I leave her, clouds

pounding, trudge back on cracked pavement,
slick with earthworms straining to the surface.

Shoreline

thins me past remembering,
past ocean's deepest gray.

My sleep, a steady
blanket smoldering

this sun, this rippled quiet.
The tide lurches on.

Persistent Roots

Come back to the tractor at the edge
of the upper lot. Come back to motor rust,
let this mud seep between
my toes and his mowing tan,
come back to root grafts, buried.

The tallest oak has lost its crown,
I hide in greening pockets, like love,
like splinters, like swollen fingertips.

When the creek refused to speak, when white
pines grew bare, my shelter fell. He drenched
his chest with baby oil, waited for new sun.
Here, an unthinking hum, the spread of dieback
disease. His breath, our branches, entwined.

Come pour my father a copper afternoon,
come grant him an ounce of ocean, dear silence,
come, let him sleep on his morphine beach.

A knife cannot
cut itself open

After the Tilt-A-Whirl

you unstrapped
the ride stopped spinning you
loved the half-dizzy haze
lingering like cotton-candy grit

before a long toke of home grown before
you slugged back another warm PBR before
you pretended to inhale

before you crashed
the Grandstand was for kids
who believed
Lipizzaner stallions were happy

to prance and pirouette whipped
in glitzy lines at the county fair in the
shrill of summer their fur a sheen

shellacked like candy apples
used to lure you like the carnies
who let you ride the roller coaster
backwards for free before

manure fog and hay
worked their way back
to the fleshy meat of your palm
cut by his suddenness

before that night you were shine
you knew the sad-eyed lambs
loved you
had to pet the 4-H piglets
sweet and horrible like saltwater taffy

all you can eat you didn't
dream him you weren't old enough
to buy PBR you try you can't

you couldn't
undo the taste of funnel cakes
or forget that night

you could not
stop his hands
tar edged towering like

the sequined jump and catch
of acrobats you saw the thin mesh
stretched beneath their trapeze

even though no one fell you
couldn't clap before you finished
the last sip of a too-blue slushie
memories stain and stick

like the press of his shadow
shivering you couldn't stop
the midway lights before you knew

these nights would forever reek
of sawdust mixed
with horse piss before he came

out of nowhere
before his switchblade
opened before

you didn't know
the heat of bleeding hands
like metal screams

in the empty talent tent he held
sharp before you knew how
to steady yourself

like water gunning be ready
before him before the bell
keep shooting
the clown's open mouth.

Writing the Lotus

We're all beasts, Sylvia.
I run like a windhorse in heat.
My poem's a stallion pounding my sheets,
days, dusks and mornings drenched in dry sweat,
wallpaper roses, repeated regrets.

Come, let's tear through the meadow,
let's canter torn lyrics, let's trample
old lies. Here in the stream, wet stones,
tadpoles and dead dragonflies.

Sylvia, I need to write flame. I need the scrape
of fall skies. I need prayers that smoke
out all the honeybees, leave me an empty hive.

My daylilies grow cold. All the petals
close against invasive ivy. Everything smells
like sonnets decomposing. I won't birth
villanelles. Won't swallow men.
This poem has to come home.

We're beasts. Watch me punch
the old pine, break my fist to find
its heartbeat. Sylvia, we're granite
shrieks with wings too broken to cry.

Hooves cleave this dry-creek bed;
my patch of dirt bleeds all over you.
Dear midwife, come hear my urge
to push out a lotus in full bloom.

The truth is our flames were never
lit. I write like a hush, like autumn's
pale sun. Sylvia, you see: my poems are
tongues buried beneath curled leaves.

Tossed

The still river rose that August
evening you lured me

like a sunfish caught
instead of trout, too small, tossed out
in court two years later, too

much work to gut you, too much
work to remember which hand
you used to open—

your switchblade tore
that night into two arms, into fury,
too much to recall where the blood began,

where my blouse ripped. Where I wouldn't
look, my eyes fixed like a fish hooked,
gills silently closing. I will never

forget your rabid breath, your lashing
tongue, unwanted. No, they weren't yours
they're mine, held tender

by the quarter moon. She churns you
in fresh river blood. A four-inch Sunny, your mud-
cut breath, lay narrow now upon this deck.

Ophidian Rising

Mother hid my pillow again. Sleep a fitful storm,
corners come undone. Each morning, a tug-of-war
to turn repeating rosebuds back where they belong.

No loose edges, no misbuttoned blouse, never slouch
in front of her or in the mirror that might speak of where—

I swim the brook of this curved ridge, here
water rules the sun. This mother realm, where
my mane of waves is not unruly, but serpentine.

In this woodland stream, no one is bent, nor
broken. Coiled joy, my back all sinew, soaring.

Mother runs her evening tub, worries
at fallen paint chips, eggshell blue.

I trail a sea of starlings to the creek
that slakes all sorrow, *Welcome back.*
My spine unwinds, molts legs and feet.

Leathery peel drops. Spun shale
shimmer. My sisters loop with me,
we splash in eddies, and no one asks

where we are or why we spin
into ourselves, eat our ends
that taste of salted rhubarb.

Riding the Ragged Edge

—You can tell a lot about a hurricane by its eye

You snapped this morning—

sapling welts, the fresh sky
sighing. Thick of my back, too forgiving.

Tomorrow I'll make you choose
my left hand.

I'll ride the heat, the stars—
these scars, an Appaloosa.

Wind shear, come. I am the gallop
of landfall, I am the new

moon lifting these cold waves.
Come darkness, come—

it's time to break this tempest.

The Crawl of Lichen

—Between every two pines is a doorway to a new world.
John Muir

Listen, the woods speak
                  his undying scent, red trillium
                  your memory-skin skittering

Welcome the wind-throw
                  his switchblade

Lie still, here in the fern bed
                  palm scars grow
                  untended

Kneel at the foot of the nurse log
                  his hewn hands;
                  eyes, sleet & hunger

Praise the new stream
                  leave no cairn

Dior and Lobster

I want a makeover. I want a tall-woman
look. I wanna speak multisyllabic Latinate. I'll toss you
words to google, since dictionaries are obsolete, and
elegant has never been my adjective.

Give me alabaster, gimme another woman's
pressed Dior, sharp wit and lipstick;
a complex fuchsia that says,
You know you want to kiss me.

Build me a new house with windows, floor-to-
nimbus. It's time to take residence in sleek, in sultry,
in self-assured. Don't bother me with keys
for fashion, glamor, bling. I'll spring that lock.

When you find me, we'll take high
tide home for supper; we'll string together
words like candied glass and philosophy.

I'm thirsty for your eyes; I'm hungry
for your nimble hips. I can't live like this,
too tentative, too cerebral.

I want out of this shelled life. I'm all torso,
boiled redder than a lobster. It's work to pull out
all this pleasure. Crack me open. Tear me tender.

Give me your buttery hands, your salt-
slick flesh. Squeeze
lemon wedges over every inch.

The sky. And the sky above that.
                The exchange of ice
between mouths.

Ode to Brigit

My head burns rhymed couplets ripped
from myth. Pastoral nightmares, curled
lips that long to taste the brim of dawn.

You snake inside my eyes,
each sestina tossed into your waves,
like knotted hair that tears my drafts back

to a whorl of tongues impossible to parse.
My mouth lined with pitted stars,
found forms like blades

of summer. We're blazed sonnets, un-
spoken. Rooms of parchment, dark-edged
reams rewritten, restless for the line that

breaks beyond the ocean floor into embryos,
birthing a garland of lotus villanelles. Let me
lay with you, Brigit, with the promise

of another evening's curve. Let me cradle
our nested lyrics. Your earlobe soft against
my chest, we swallow daylight.

Sea of Origami Birds

Our arms, our hips, our stolen sighs with no care
for art or food. Promises slip from a silk duvet we tear
through days, spill into the sky unstained

by night's sweet hush—rings on a windowsill, pale stains.
Lost in a pillow sham of Italian lace, sewn into knotted care.
We're two buttonholes, taut seams we tear

the world into one scent like a summer rain torn
from unspoken storms, our backs curling stained
secrets, we swallow ourselves inside a sea uncaring,

salt of careless nights. riptide. bare stain.

After I Fell

into his uneasy rains, our sweet toxins surfaced.

I barreled into his
baritone. Buttery. And convincing.

His hand on my thigh, a constant I craved,
trail of his fingers, small of my back, dawn sweat.

He cried. Miles deep. Without explanation.

When he fed me avocados with his fingers, that's when I knew, or started to.

He sniffed his hands while driving. At the movies, he jackhammered our entire row.
       This can't be stopped.

He hummed while ironing. Pitchy and repeating. There was a wife who said,
       He scared me.

He was creme brulee, manhattans, filet mignon. No cigarettes or children—yet.

When he said, *I was just flirting*, I traded my sour for his hazels, their midnight swim.
       Hello love.

He washed my hair in our corner shower. His hands, delicate and kind. His divorce
papers mentioned throwing kitchen things.

When I told him in a whisper, *I want to have your babies*,
       he didn't disappear.

When I said, *I dreamt our newborn was too tiny to feed*, he read
to me Bahá'u'lláh, his cadence steady.

I wrote horrible love poems. He kept them all. Wrinkled scrap, wildflowers,
       night shimmer.

At our friend's memorial, we danced in church, in yesterday's incense, in prismed light, in front of Mary, even if we shouldn't have
        —we danced.

Punto in Aria

In the dim of one thousand mornings
we're knotted, not quite summer

more like an early mist
drunk on day lilies tipping

light into lace,
set free of scaffolds.

We left parchment
nights stained

screams inside
fingers, folded wishes.

We were stitched seams lifted
like an old pattern torn—

twitching heat, your evening
hands, iron spun in swells

you tamped
with fists and left

my arms aching to cage
each surge with a safety lock.

Our eyes lit by the blood moon,
we hide in a rent of lace.

You taste like daylight,
a dozen long-stem reds,

balloons that said
Get Well Soon.

All 8,294,400 Pixels Point in the Same Direction

I want a divorce from dusk Annul this ache I want to but you don't want to fall awake
I want skin-dreamt arms Give me pinpricks in the evening ceiling I want Orion to pierce
my tongue I want to feel the glint of morning in my fingers I want a promise but you can't
stop telling me there are no guarantees I want a fool-proof warranty but you won't
I want my money back I want to burn every cushion on our couch ·   I want to kill the TV
I can't you won't I want fire-toasted eyes for breakfast smothered in ghost peppers Gimme
bottled daylight I want it straight up I want to pour another I want to break your purple lava
lamp and let all the lavender ooze between my toes screaming   IT'S NOT A DREAM
I want the sun volume on full blast but I know you won't like it when the ceiling fan starts to
wobble laugh I want to lick storm clouds and leave only light I want to learn the cha-cha
                    barefoot in fresh-cut grass
                          open all the windows
                              throw out the remote

Half Life

When you die, where will we meet?
Will you wake me with tinny shouts *eh eh uh*?
Your fisticuffs, the devil's head, you have to—
his pronged tongue, a captious hiss.

You remember him, the crack of the hemlock.
When you die, if we meet, will the soft dent
of your pillow feel repeated? Will I forget
our lips, our legs, our yesterdays, will your hands

speak to me of first love, avocado slivers? When our hips
give way to soil, our toes, like hungry ants, will file inside
these peony-drunk petals. When you die, we'll meet
in dreams of stamen nectar. You didn't mean to

punch my cheek, you were kerosene when you hit.
Dolls hang from strings above our bed. When I snap
their plastic heads, our room smells giddy. The wind,
umami. When you die, come find me in the peonies.

Shoveled Tea

—after William Shakespeare

Our love
tastes watery. Today it is
not the warm broth I remember, not
your long glance pouring love
into chipped porcelain, which
cools like a thick sigh that alters
who we are—is never who we were when
we met—your eyes, my every breath. It
grew bitter in alterations,
empty cups, spilled cream. I find
us stuck to the bottom of a sugar bowl, or
perhaps we're waiting for what bends
these night walls, what stirs affection with
a murmur, wakes us in the
chill of morning? What remover
eclipsed our once abiding sun? It's difficult to
choose which cup to remove.

Naiad's Den

You came here to drown
those silken nights. Any sea nymph

could smell the skin you wear,
still tangled in your lover's hair.

You came here to cast off
whispers that linger

on your lips, like a razor
cut, too thin. Descend—

my love, this squid-ink
haze will hold you. Give me

the days you tossed
to the edge of forgetting.

There's only this witching
sleep, these cave drums calling—

dear mothwing, let me
lick these shallows,

my tongue, your salt cuts.

When the Ending Begins

I left your wall of waves to lay among
young birches, spoon moss pillows.

Bed of ferns, no sting. Spring rains,
my feet, fresh violets.

I warned the fawn—
don't sip from that empty well.

When I kissed a pink lady slipper,
she didn't ask.

the river turned white
before you were born

You Asked Me Why

your father and I didn't stop—
your myelin sheath
began unfurling

with my father, my brother,
your uncle, your papa's eyes
emptying galaxies

with whiskey, with weed,
with washboard clouds
that scrub me, sudden and fresh.

I believe in being swallowed.
I believe in distant rust, in metal links
anchoring me to you, to imperfect serotonin.

I'll never muster enough
to dispel your heritable itch,
this tattered summer—

where my father drank bourbon for breakfast,
where you lost your fourth kindergarten coat,
where my brother slung smack.

We're frayed synapses,
we're misfired laughter,
asymmetry—

                the blue behind
our broken sky. You tell me
you don't want babies.

Bodhisattva Curtains

You slip beneath the river's boil line.
How your father started all those years ago, I can't—
Let me give you my arms. I owe you more than these
two hands, more than river sticks, tadpoles, flawed love.
I read texts extolling patience, my hair on fire, I meditate.
Was it only once, dear daughter?

I sewed you an ivory canopy, bed curtains
trimmed in lace. Yellow now, my love.

My light flickers unreliably. I stumble
the mud-strewn bank. Armless, I can't
swim through these crayfish, unspoken boulders.
Make my torso your ghost boat, tear me across
these washboard arguments, glass eels. Did you hide,
cornered in a fort of crooked chairs, torn wool?
Did his storm quell while I walked? I prayed
for rain. The texts suggest slapping my arms.

I sewed you an ivory canopy, bed curtains
trimmed in lace. Yellow now, my love. And tangled.

Dear daughter, was it only once? The texts speak
of love that lingers like lavender on fingertips,
like your one-dimple kiss. Let this river take me,
take all the shadows I tried to drown
that evening. Knees to lichen, I begged
the young birch—brave rain, petals in your palm.

Wider Aperture, a Mother's Study

—There are always two people in every picture:
the photographer and the viewer. Ansel Adams

i

let's find your newborn
breath
sweet pinpricks
the soft of my palm

let's find old afternoons
scooch of wooly worms
mostly orange
please

ii

your self portrait
a texture study with cornered walls
shudders me, your arms
hung themselves

iii

I know you didn't mean to
expose your razored-ankle scars,
my shins ache
inside

let's find another
bright-winged tiger moth
as long as it lives,
please

Cairn in a Pillowcase

My mind's a large cat,
caged and sleepless. Bloodstones,
my throat, a cavern keening.

Your juice box, a center dent, unyielding keening—
tugs like summer, like our calico
licking rounded bloodstones.

Where do we bury broken bloodstones—
laughter? Knot deep my keening,
take this stained pillowcase, unwanted kittens.

Toss me to these river cats. Bloodstones, sink this keening.

The Duel

In first grade he sits on his
coat. Ignores the cubby because
some part of him wants a cushion—

a cushion between school
and home, where his family understands
that he will pull a loose string,

pull the thread to its enticing beginning
and if that means a seam unravels
and if that makes his cubby oddly empty—

he revels in an empty space,
fills it with a stash of paper clips,
builds towers, odd angles everywhere

a ticking clock, hands angled left then right
and back to the tidy scent of his
teacher's hair, her heels so brisk she breaks

his polychrome, broken by her nails
tapping his desk where he launches
his hero pen. *Choose your weapon now*, he tells

himself, *Not now*. Now is two hands on his shoulders.
Now is math stations. Now is get your assignments.
Cascading papers, chicken scratched, fly

to the floor, battlefield of paper, pencil gallops,
sword raised; she closes in. *Where is your work?*
Now. Not now. Now work. Now choose. Now.

This Art Has Eyes

—After viewing a digital reproduction of Munch's *The Scream*

strung in a series of   zeros & ones

vectored   perhaps corrupted

parameters   can't art solve for

null   impulses

auto   generated

we crave   encrypted

fiber optic   blends we smoke

someone else's   source code

our content   blocked

by polygons   pixelated

we're buried   in ungessoed white

we're auto   fractals

fire in a microwave   abandoned motherboards

unbleached sun

i trail you crisscrossing
fallen sticks make

perfect sense your
house sings like spring

peepers live with
ice in their bellies surviving

sumac hides a hall connecting
our old home to this

tub's swimming
floors spin my

teeth taste like
gritty sugar mix

me with two eggs
a kitchen table's broken leg

like cricket wishes with no walls
to scrub no sheets to bleach

you grin coatless
open like a winter pine

When You Turn Thirty

I want to wean you
see I need
another mother

to feed me warm
syrup in a bottle if you
suck the marrow from

osso bucco bones they
drip like laughter dipped
in sting. I want some days

primrose.
Tuck you in a bed
of tulip sun before

the ocean pulls you
are my impacted tooth
your smile should be summer

sands bury me, leave
the smallest oval, a breath,
a pocket of sky.

Be the Quelling Breeze

Come cross this thunder, cross this snaking river
at its fire head. Cut the tail of derecho winds—
come be the unbroken branch.

Consider the lilacs, their mooning boughs,
too trusting. Cross again, these nettled waters—
for the simple blooms, make yourself a quelling breeze,

a knowing oak. Bend against clawed gusts,
root and sun. Hold your long branch
steady. Wait like the clay bottom of an old river—

be the cloudless brook, the softest gust; lay safe the young boughs.

Set the Clocks Back

Why do I always go to Heron Rock?
It's just a cove. I need a new song, a new
poem to drown me. I want to run away.

I want to shout into the mouth of the river.
Break its taut skin. There are probably still PCBs,
bottom sludge, invasive species,

water chestnuts that slice the bottom
of your feet. When we were kids,
we called them Chinese prickers.

We swam in sneakers, didn't know
water nuts are good for diabetes and catfish
store toxins in their fat. We knew the smell

of a rainstorm coming, the sway of a poplar.
Every year we set the clocks back, lose sun
to October's claw. She carries me

in her half-dead light, empties
my family into potholes and complicated
mud ruts that look like last week's leftovers.

We need supper. I'll dig up my cord,
sauté it with garlic. Nobody eats shad fish
anymore, too many worries, like love or chicken

not fully cooked, like my son's PTSD stuck
between two sticks of butter, baking soda box.
We'll eat again. Click the plastic shut.

Ars Poetica, No. 10 Hooks

You gotta know your sunfish. Me?
I like 'em small. Feel for the first tug.
Don't let 'em get around your bait.

Use live lures. Little bitty hooks,
No. 6 & 10 work best. Or try them
wire shanks, the thin ones. Trust me.

Pulling out that tiny mouth, it's a messy
proposition. Ya haveta handle 'em
real gentle. See how delicate the flesh is?

I'll tell you a secret—wait for rain.
They come up hungry. Cover your hook
with just enough lure, and she's yours.

No weight, no fight at all. Another man
might toss 'em, back, but when I hook
a young one too deep, I keep her.

Dear Mother of Beauty

Show me how ruin makes
a home. It has been so wet;
stones glaze in moss; everything blooms
coldly. Allow me to sit in the sun and listen
to the sky. Gently, I wear
a torn place on my sleeve.

Notes

"a towel hangs from a line / a sheet of iron in the sky" is from Nick Flynn's "My Mother Contemplating Her Gun."

The refrain in "Fresh Eggs for Mama" is from James Schuyler's "Buried at Springs."

"a piece breaks off, / declares itself" is from Valerio Magrelli's "[I Love Uncertain Gestures]." Translated by Dana Gioia.

"Your Lilacs Nest in Me" adapts lines from Walt Whitman's "When Lilacs Last in the Dooryard Bloom'd," "A Noiseless Patient Spider" and "Song of Myself." The following works by Vincent van Gogh are referenced: *Birds' Nest*, *Irises* and *Wheat Field with Cypresses*.

"A knife cannot cut itself open" is from Jane Hirshfield's "Assay Only Glimpsable for an Instant."

"Shoveled Tea" is a golden shovel drawn from William Shakespeare's "Sonnet 116": "Love is not love / which alters when it alterations find, / Or bends with the remover to remove."

"The sky. And the sky above that. The exchange of ice between mouths" is from Rebecca Lindenberg's "Poetic Subjects."

Punto in aria translates as *stitched in air*. An Italian lace that breaks free of its binding.

"the river turned white / before you were born" is from W.S. Merwin's "Wanting to See."

"Dear Mother of Beauty" is a cento composed of lines from Ocean Vuong's "A Little Closer to the Edge," Lisa Olstein's "Dear One Absent This Long While," Chungmi Kim's "Allow Me" and W.S. Merwin's "The Nails." Title is after Wallace Stevens' "Sunday Morning."

Acknowledgments

Anti-Heroin Chic	"Did You See Him"
Arsenic Lobster	"Dog Flowers"
ArtAscent	"Skate Me a River"
Artemis Journal	"Naiad's Den"
Boyne Berries	"What Lingers"
Chronogram	"Before We Burned"
Clackamas Literary Review	"Your Lilacs Nest in Me"
Coe Review	"Petals"
Grub Street	"Persistent Roots"
Guide to Kultur	"On the Pond," "Skimming Stones"
January Review	"Half Life," "Tossed," "Jellyfish in June"
Mom Egg Review	"Egg Shells"
New Reader Magazine	"Fresh Eggs for Mama," "The Duel," "Loose Gravel"
Rat's Ass Review	"Ode to Brigit"
River Heron Review	"Shoveled Tea," "Dior and Lobster"
Sequestrum	"All 8,294,400 Pixels Point in the Same Direction," "Sea of Origami Birds"
Two Thirds North	"Punto in Aria"
Up The River	"Shoreline"

Title Index

First Line Index

Y

www.ingramcontent.com/pod-product-compliance
Lightning Source LLC
Chambersburg PA
CBHW010857090426

42737CB00020B/3410